TABLE OF CONTENTS

PAGE 4

INTRODUCTION

Background and Benefits

PAGE 6

GUIDELINES

General Rules and Principles

PAGE 8

BREAKFAST RECIPES

15 Recipes for Breakfast Delights

PAGE 26

LUNCH RECIPES

15 Recipes for Happy Lunch

PAGE 44

DINNER RECIPES

20 Recipes for Dinner Magic

PAGE 66

DESSERT RECIPES

15 Recipes for Dessert Bliss

INTRODUCTION

BACKGROUND
WHAT IS THE DR NOWZARADAN DIET?

MY STORY
THIS DIET SAVE MY LIFE!

GUIDELINES
GENERAL RULES AND PRINCIPLES

WHAT IS THE DR NOWZARADAN'S DIET?

Welcome to the Dr Nowzaradan Diet Cookbook, a guide to help you lose weight and improve your health with delicious and nutritious recipes. Whether you are preparing for weight loss surgery, or simply want to adopt a healthier lifestyle, this cookbook will provide you with the tools and inspiration you need to succeed.

The Birth of the Diet

The Dr Nowzaradan Diet is a low-calorie, low-carbohydrate diet that was developed by Dr Younan Nowzaradan, a renowned bariatric surgeon who has helped hundreds of patients with morbid obesity on the reality show "My 600-Lb. Life." The diet aims to promote rapid weight loss before surgery by limiting the intake of sugar, fat, and starchy vegetables. The diet consists of small servings of real food, such as lean protein, non-starchy vegetables, salads, and whole grains.

Benefits

The benefits of following this diet are not only physical, but also mental and emotional. Many people who have followed this diet have reported improved self-esteem, confidence, mood, and quality of life. They have also overcome various health issues related to obesity, such as diabetes, hypertension, sleep apnea, joint pain, and more.

However, this diet is not for everyone. It is very restrictive and should only be attempted under medical supervision. It can also have some potential side effects, such as fatigue, hunger, headaches, nausea, and constipation. Therefore, it is important to consult your doctor before starting this diet and follow their advice closely.

MY LIFE WITH THE DIET

My personal motivation for writing this cookbook is to share my own experience with the Dr Nowzaradan Diet and how it changed my life for the better.

I was 542 pounds...
I was 542 pounds when I decided to undergo weight loss surgery with Dr Now. He put me on his diet plan and I managed to lose 342 pounds in two years. I feel happier and healthier than ever before. I also discovered a passion for cooking and creating new recipes that fit the diet.

I was not always obese. I was a normal weight until I got married and had three children. My husband was also overweight and we enabled each other's unhealthy eating habits. We ate a lot of fast food, junk food, and processed food. We rarely cooked at home or ate any fruits or vegetables. We also did not exercise or do any physical activity. Our lifestyle took a toll on our health and our relationship. We both developed diabetes, high blood pressure, high cholesterol, and sleep apnea. We also had low self-esteem, depression, and anxiety. We argued a lot and were unhappy with ourselves and each other.

The turning point came when my husband died at 33 from a heart attack. He weighed over 600 pounds at the time. I was devastated and scared for my own life and my children's future. I knew I had to make a big change or I would end up like him.

That's when I contacted Dr Now...
That's when I contacted Dr Now and applied for weight loss surgery. He accepted me as his patient but told me that I had to lose 50 pounds on my own before he could operate on me. He gave me his diet plan and told me to follow it strictly.

I did as he said and lost 50 pounds in three months and qualified for surgery. Dr Now performed a gastric bypass on me and removed most of my stomach. He told me that the surgery was only a tool and that I had to continue following his diet plan after the surgery.

Two years after surgery, I reached my goal weight of 200 pounds. I lost a total of 342 pounds or more than half of my body weight. I was overjoyed and grateful for his help and guidance. He saved my life and gave me a new one. He also inspired me to help others who are struggling with obesity and want to lose weight.

That's why I decided to write this cookbook and share my story with you. I want to show you that it is possible to follow the Dr Nowzaradan Diet and achieve your weight loss goals. I want to share with you some of the recipes that helped me along the way.

I hope this cookbook will help you lose weight!

RULES AND PRINCIPLES

Before you start cooking and enjoying the recipes in this cookbook, you need to know some basic guidelines on how to follow the Dr Nowzaradan Diet.

This diet is very restrictive and should only be attempted under medical supervision. It can also have some potential side effects, such as fatigue, hunger, headaches, nausea, and constipation. Therefore, it is important to consult your doctor before starting this diet and follow their advice closely.

The main goal of this diet is to help you lose weight quickly by cutting your calorie intake to around 1200 calories per day. However, this does not mean that you can eat anything you want as long as it fits within your calorie limit. You also need to pay attention to the types and amounts of food you eat, and make sure that your diet is balanced and nutritious.

Here are some general rules and principles of the Dr Nowzaradan Diet:

Eat two to three meals per day with no snacks

Dr Nowzaradan recommends eating two to three meals per day with no snacks in between. This helps you control your appetite and avoid overeating. You should also avoid skipping meals or fasting, as this can slow down your metabolism and make you more likely to binge later.

Divide your calories evenly among your meals

You should aim to consume around 400 calories for each meal if you eat three times a day, or 600 calories for each meal if you eat twice a day. This helps you keep your blood sugar levels stable and prevent cravings. You should also avoid eating too late at night or too close to bedtime, as this can interfere with your sleep quality and hormone balance.

Avoid sugar and choose low-carb foods

. Sugar is one of the main enemies of this diet, as it can spike your blood sugar levels, increase your appetite, and cause inflammation. You should avoid all forms of sugar, including honey, maple syrup, agave nectar, fruit juice, soda, candy, cake, cookies, ice cream, etc. You should also limit your intake of starchy vegetables, such as potatoes, corn, peas, carrots, etc., as they are high in carbs and calories. Instead, choose low-carb foods that are high in fiber and water content, such as leafy greens, broccoli, cauliflower, cabbage, zucchini, etc.

Drink plenty of water and avoid sugary drinks
Water is essential for your health and weight loss. It helps you stay hydrated, flush out toxins, regulate your body temperature, lubricate your joints, improve your skin quality, and prevent constipation. You should drink at least 8 glasses of water per day or more if you exercise or sweat a lot. You should also avoid sugary drinks such as soda (even diet soda), fruit juice (even 100% juice), sports drinks (even sugar-free ones), energy drinks (even sugar-free ones), etc., as they can add unnecessary calories and chemicals to your diet. Instead, drink water, unsweetened tea, coffee (without cream or sugar), or low-fat milk.

Take a multivitamin and mineral supplement daily
Because this diet is very low in calories and some food groups, you may not get enough vitamins and minerals from your food alone. Therefore, it is important to take a multivitamin and mineral supplement every day to prevent deficiencies and support your health. You should consult your doctor or dietitian about the best type and dose of supplement for you.

Monitor your weight and blood sugar levels regularly
This diet can help you lose weight quickly, but it can also affect your blood sugar levels. If you have diabetes or prediabetes, you should monitor your blood sugar levels regularly and adjust your medication accordingly. You should also weigh yourself once a week and keep track of your progress. If you notice any unusual symptoms or side effects, such as dizziness, weakness, nausea, or chest pain, you should contact your doctor immediately.

These are some of the basic guidelines on how to follow the Dr Nowzaradan Diet. However, keep in mind that this diet is not a one-size-fits-all solution. You may need to modify it according to your individual needs, preferences, and medical conditions. You should always consult your doctor or dietitian before starting this diet and follow their recommendations.

Enjoy!

CONTENT

1. Veggie Omelette — 10
2. Greek Yogurt Parfait — 11
3. Spinach and Mushroom Frittata — 12
4. Quinoa Breakfast Bowl — 13
5. Smoked Salmon and Avocado Toast — 14
6. Berry Protein Smoothie — 15
7. Egg White Scramble with Turkey Bacon — 16
8. Chia Seed Pudding with Berries — 17
9. Cottage Cheese Pancakes — 18
10. Vegetable Breakfast Burrito — 19
11. Baked Egg Cups with Spinach and Tomato — 20
12. Almond Flour Pancakes — 21
13. Sweet Potato Hash with Eggs — 22
14. Green Smoothie Bowl — 23
15. Egg Muffins with Spinach and Feta — 24

VEGGIE OMELETTE

1 serving | 10 mins | 15 mins

Start your day with a protein-packed omelette filled with an assortment of colorful and nutritious vegetables.

Ingredients

- 2 large eggs
- 1/4 cup water
- Salt and pepper, to taste
- Olive oil spray
- 1/4 cup diced red onion
- 1/4 cup diced green bell pepper
- 1/4 cup sliced mushrooms
- 1/4 cup chopped spinach
- 2 tbsps shredded cheddar cheese

Instructions

1. In a small bowl, whisk together the eggs, water, salt, and pepper until well combined and frothy. Set aside.
2. Heat a medium nonstick skillet over medium-high heat and lightly spray with olive oil spray. Add the onion, bell pepper, and mushrooms and cook, stirring occasionally, for about 10 minutes, or until soft and browned. Transfer the veggies to a plate and keep warm.
3. Wipe the skillet clean and spray again with olive oil spray. Reduce the heat to medium-low and pour in the egg mixture. Cook for about 5 minutes, or until the edges are set and the center is slightly runny.
4. Sprinkle the cheese over half of the omelette and top with the veggie mixture. Fold the other half of the omelette over the filling and gently press to seal.
5. Carefully slide the omelette onto a serving plate and enjoy!

Nutrients (per serving)

Calories: 300   Protein: 23g   Fat: 18g   Carbohydrates: 12g   Fiber: 3g   Sugar: 0g

GREEK YOGURT PARFAIT

🍴 1 serving   🕐 5 mins    0 min

Indulge in a creamy and satisfying parfait layered with Greek yogurt, fresh berries, and a sprinkle of crunchy granola.

Ingredients

- 1/2 cup plain Greek yogurt, full fat
- 1 tbsp sugar-free honey substitute (such as Nature's Hollow)
- 1/4 tsp vanilla extract
- 1/4 cup fresh or frozen blueberries
- 2 tbsps sliced almonds

Instructions

1. In a small bowl, stir together the yogurt, honey substitute, and vanilla extract until well combined and smooth.
2. In a glass or jar, layer half of the yogurt mixture, followed by half of the blueberries and half of the almonds. Repeat with the remaining yogurt, blueberries, and almonds.
3. Enjoy immediately or refrigerate until ready to eat.

Nutrients (per serving)

Calories: 250   Protein: 17g   Fat: 15g   Carbohydrates: 15g   Fiber: 3g   Sugar: 8g

SPINACH & MUSH-ROOM FRITTATA

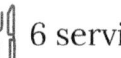 6 servings   🕐 10 mins   40 mins

Enjoy a flavorful frittata made with nutrient-rich spinach and earthy mushrooms, perfect for a hearty and healthy breakfast.

Ingredients

- 8 large eggs
- 1/4 cup heavy cream
- Salt and pepper, to taste
- Olive oil spray
- 2 cups fresh spinach, chopped
- 1 cup sliced mushrooms
- 1/4 cup shredded mozzarella cheese
- 2 tbsps grated parmesan cheese

Instructions

1. Preheat oven to 375°F and lightly spray a 9-inch pie dish with olive oil spray. Set aside.
2. In a large bowl, whisk together the eggs, cream, salt, and pepper until well combined and frothy. Set aside.
3. Heat a large skillet over medium-high heat and spray with olive oil spray. Add the spinach and mushrooms and cook, stirring occasionally, for about 15 minutes, or until wilted and browned. Drain any excess liquid and transfer the veggies to the prepared pie dish. Spread them evenly over the bottom of the dish.
4. Pour the egg mixture over the veggies and sprinkle with mozzarella and parmesan cheese.
5. Bake for 25 to 30 minutes, or until the frittata is set and golden on top.
6. Let it rest for 10 minutes before slicing and serving.

Nutrients (per serving)

Calories: 210   Protein: 15g   Fat: 15g   Carbohydrates: 3g   Fiber: 0.5g   Sugar: 1.5g

QUINOA BREAK-FAST BOWL

 1 serving   🕒 5 mins    15 mins

Energize your morning with a nourishing bowl of quinoa, topped with your favorite fruits, nuts, and a drizzle of honey.

Ingredients

- 1/2 cup uncooked quinoa
- 1 cup water
- 1/4 tsp salt
- 1/4 tsp cinnamon
- 1/4 cup unsweetened almond milk
- 1/4 cup fresh or frozen blueberries
- 2 tbsps sliced almonds
- 2 tsps sugar-free honey substitute

Instructions

1. Rinse the quinoa well under cold water and drain. Add the quinoa, water, salt, and cinnamon to a small saucepan and bring to a boil. Reduce the heat and simmer, covered, for about 15 minutes, or until the quinoa is fluffy and the water is absorbed. Fluff with a fork and set aside.
2. In a small microwave-safe bowl, heat the almond milk for about 30 seconds, or until warm.
3. In another small microwave-safe bowl, heat the blueberries for about 30 seconds, or until thawed and juicy.
4. Divide the quinoa between two bowls and drizzle with the almond milk. Top with the blueberries, almonds, and honey substitute. Enjoy!

Nutrients (per serving)

Calories: 250   Protein: 9g   Fat: 8g   Carbohydrates: 37g   Fiber: 6g   Sugar: 7g

SMOKED SALMON & AVOCADO TOAST

🍴 4 servings   🕐 10 mins   🔥 5 mins

Elevate your toast game with a delightful combination of smoked salmon, creamy avocado, and a squeeze of lemon for a refreshing start to your day.

Ingredients

- 4 slices of whole-wheat bread
- 1 ripe avocado, peeled and pitted
- 2 tsps of lemon juice
- Salt and pepper, to taste
- 4 ounces of smoked salmon
- 2 tbsps of chopped fresh dill

Instructions

1. Toast the bread slices until golden and crisp. Set aside.
2. In a small bowl, mash the avocado with a fork until smooth. Stir in the lemon juice and season with salt and pepper to taste.
3. Spread the avocado mixture evenly over the toast slices. Top each with smoked salmon and sprinkle with dill.
4. Cut each toast in half and serve.

Nutrients (per serving)

Calories: 240   Protein: 14g   Fat: 11g   Carbohydrates: 25g   Fiber: 6g   Sugar: 4g

BERRY PROTEIN SMOOTHIE

 1 serving   5 mins    0 min

Blend together a refreshing and protein-packed smoothie using your favorite berries and a scoop of protein powder for a nutritious and convenient breakfast on the go.

Ingredients

- 1 cup unsweetened almond milk
- 1/4 cup fresh or frozen mixed berries (such as blueberries, raspberries, and blackberries)
- 1 scoop vanilla protein powder
- 2 tsps sugar-free honey substitute
- 1/4 tsp vanilla extract
- A few ice cubes

Instructions

1. Add all the ingredients to a blender and blend until smooth and frothy.
2. Pour into a glass and enjoy!

Nutrients (per serving)

Calories: 180   Protein: 23g   Fat: 5g   Carbohydrates: 12g   Fiber: 3g   Sugar: 6g

EGG WHITE SCRAMBLE WITH TURKEY BACON

🍴 4 servings   🕐 10 mins   🔥 30 mins

Enjoy a lighter twist on a classic scramble by using egg whites and pairing them with flavorful turkey bacon.

Ingredients

- 4 slices of turkey bacon
- 1/4 cup chopped onion
- 1/4 cup chopped green bell pepper
- 1/4 cup chopped mushroom
- 6 egg whites
- Salt and pepper, to taste
- 2 tbsps shredded cheddar cheese
- Fresh parsley, for garnish (optional)

Instructions

1. In a large nonstick skillet over medium-high heat, cook the turkey bacon until crisp, turning occasionally, for about 10 minutes. Transfer to a paper towel-lined plate and chop into small pieces. Set aside.
2. In the same skillet over medium-high heat, cook the onion, bell pepper, and mushroom, stirring occasionally, until soft and browned, for about 15 minutes. Transfer to a bowl and keep warm.
3. In a small bowl, whisk the egg whites with salt and pepper until well combined and frothy.
4. Spray the same skillet with cooking spray and heat over medium-low heat. Pour in the egg whites and cook, stirring occasionally, until set, for about 5 minutes.
5. Stir in the cheese and turkey bacon and cook until cheese is melted, for about 1 minute.
6. Divide the egg white scramble among four plates and top with the vegetable mixture. Garnish with parsley if desired and serve.

Nutrients (per serving)

Calories: 160   Protein: 19g   Fat: 7g   Carbohydrates: 5g   Fiber: 1g   Sugar: 2g

CHIA SEED PUDD-ING WITH BERRIES

🍴 2 servings   🕐 5 mins   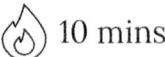 10 mins

Delight in a creamy chia seed pudding infused with your choice of milk and topped with a medley of vibrant berries.

Ingredients

- 1/4 cup chia seeds
- 1 cup unsweetened almond milk
- 2 tsps sugar-free honey substitute (such as Nature's Hollow)
- 1/4 tsp vanilla extract
- 1/4 cup fresh or frozen mixed berries (such as blueberries, raspberries, and blackberries)

Instructions

1. In a small bowl, whisk together the chia seeds, almond milk, honey substitute, and vanilla extract until well combined. Cover and refrigerate for at least 4 hours or overnight, until the chia seeds have absorbed the liquid and formed a thick pudding-like texture.
2. In a small saucepan over low heat, cook the berries, stirring occasionally, until soft and juicy, for about 10 minutes. You can also microwave them for about 2 minutes, if you prefer.
3. Spoon the chia pudding into a bowl and top with the berry sauce. Enjoy cold or warm.

Nutrients (per serving)

Calories: 170   Protein: 6g   Fat: 9g   Carbohydrates: 18g   Fiber: 3g   Sugar: 6g

COTTAGE CHEESE PANCAKES

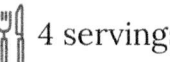 4 servings   10 mins    15 mins

Delight in a creamy chia seed pudding infused with your choice of milk and topped with a medley of vibrant berries.

Ingredients

- 1 cup low-fat cottage cheese
- 4 eggs
- 1/4 cup almond flour
- Cooking spray
- 2 tsps sugar-free honey substitute (such as Nature's Hollow)
- 1/4 tsp baking powder
- 1/4 tsp vanilla extract

Instructions

1. In a blender or food processor, combine the cottage cheese, eggs, honey substitute, and vanilla extract. Blend until smooth and creamy.
2. Add the almond flour and baking powder and blend again until well combined.
3. Heat a large nonstick skillet over medium-high heat and lightly spray with cooking spray. Drop about 1/4 cup of batter per pancake onto the skillet and cook for about 3 minutes per side, or until golden and cooked through.
4. Repeat with the remaining batter, spraying the skillet as needed.
5. Serve the pancakes with your favorite toppings, such as fresh berries, sugar-free jam, or whipped cream.

Nutrients (per serving)

Calories: 200   Protein: 18g   Fat: 11g   Carbohydrates: 8g   Fiber: 2g   Sugar: 4g

VEGETABLE BREAK FAST BURRITO

🍴 4 servings 🕐 10 mins 🔥 25 mins

Wrap up a nutritious and delicious breakfast by filling a whole-grain tortilla with a medley of sautéed vegetables and a sprinkle of cheese.

Ingredients

- 4 whole-wheat tortillas
- 4 eggs
- 1/4 cup low-fat milk
- Salt and pepper, to taste
- Cooking spray
- 1/2 cup chopped onion
- 1/2 cup chopped red bell pepper
- 1/2 cup chopped mushroom
- 1/4 tsp cumin
- 1/4 tsp paprika
- 1/4 tsp garlic powder
- 1/4 cup shredded cheddar cheese
- 1/4 cup salsa

Instructions

1. In a small bowl, whisk together the eggs, milk, salt, and pepper until well combined. Set aside.
2. Heat a large nonstick skillet over medium-high heat and spray with cooking spray. Add the onion, bell pepper, mushroom, cumin, paprika, and garlic powder and cook, stirring occasionally, until soft and browned, for about 15 minutes.
3. Reduce the heat to medium-low and pour in the egg mixture. Cook, stirring occasionally, until the eggs are set, for about 10 minutes.
4. Warm the tortillas in a microwave or oven until soft and pliable.
5. Divide the egg and vegetable mixture among the tortillas and sprinkle with cheese. Fold the bottom edge of each tortilla over the filling, then fold in the sides and roll up tightly.
6. Serve the burritos with salsa on the side or drizzled over the top.

Nutrients (per serving)

Calories: 280   Protein: 17g   Fat: 11g   Carbohydrates: 30g   Fiber: 5g   Sugar: 6g

BAKED EGG CUPS WITH SPINACH & TOMATO

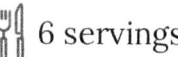 6 servings 10 mins  20 mins

Bake savory egg cups filled with nutritious spinach and juicy tomatoes for a convenient grab-and-go breakfast option.

Ingredients

- Cooking spray
- 4 cups fresh baby spinach
- 1 cup cherry tomatoes, halved
- Salt and pepper, to taste
- 8 eggs
- 1/4 cup grated parmesan cheese
- 2 tbsps chopped fresh basil

Instructions

1. Preheat oven to 375°F and lightly spray a 12-cup muffin tin with cooking spray. Set aside.
2. In a large skillet over medium-high heat, cook the spinach, stirring occasionally, until wilted, for about 5 minutes. Drain any excess liquid and divide the spinach among the prepared muffin cups, pressing lightly to make a well in the center.
3. Place two tomato halves on top of each spinach layer and season with salt and pepper.
4. Carefully crack an egg into a small bowl and slide it into one of the spinach wells. Repeat with the remaining eggs.
5. Sprinkle the parmesan cheese and basil over the egg cups.
6. Bake for 15 to 20 minutes, or until the eggs are cooked to your liking.
7. Let the egg cups cool slightly before removing from the muffin tin. Enjoy warm or at room temperature.

Nutrients (per serving)

Calories: 140   Protein: 13g   Fat: 8g   Carbohydrates: 3g   Fiber: 1g   Sugar: 1g

ALMOND FLOUR PANCAKES

 4 servings   🕐 10 mins    15 mins

Enjoy light and fluffy pancakes made with almond flour, a gluten-free alternative that adds a nutty flavor and extra nutrients.

Ingredients

- 1 1/2 cups blanched almond flour
- 2 tsps baking powder
- 1/4 tsp salt
- 3 eggs
- 1/4 cup unsweetened almond milk
- 2 tbsps oil (such as avocado oil or melted coconut oil)
- 1 tsp vanilla extract
- Optional: blueberries or sugar-free chocolate chips

Instructions

1. In a large bowl, whisk together the almond flour, baking powder, and salt until well combined. Set aside.
2. In a medium bowl, whisk together the eggs, almond milk, oil, and vanilla extract until well combined.
3. Add the wet ingredients to the dry ingredients and mix well until a smooth batter forms. If using blueberries or chocolate chips, fold them in gently.
4. Heat a large nonstick skillet over medium-low heat and lightly grease with oil or cooking spray. Drop about 1/4 cup of batter per pancake onto the skillet and cook for about 3 minutes, or until bubbles form on the surface. Flip and cook for another 2 minutes, or until golden and cooked through.
5. Repeat with the remaining batter, greasing the skillet as needed.
6. Serve the pancakes with your favorite toppings, such as sugar-free syrup, whipped cream, butter, or more berries.

Nutrients (per serving)

Calories: 370   Protein: 15g   Fat: 31g   Carbohydrates: 11g   Fiber: 5g   Sugar: 2g

SWEET POTATO HASH WITH EGGS

 4 servings   🕐 15 mins   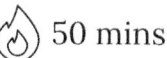 50 mins

Savor a hearty and wholesome breakfast by combining roasted sweet potatoes with perfectly cooked eggs for a satisfying start to your day.

Ingredients

- 2 medium sweet potatoes, peeled and diced into 1/2 inch cubes
- 4 slices of bacon, chopped
- 1/4 cup chopped onion
- 1/4 cup chopped red bell pepper
- Salt and pepper, to taste
- 4 cups chopped kale
- 4 eggs

Instructions

1. Preheat oven to 375°F and lightly spray a baking sheet with cooking spray. Spread the sweet potato cubes in an even layer on the prepared baking sheet. Bake for 15 minutes, or until tender and slightly browned.
2. In a large oven-safe skillet over medium-high heat, cook the bacon, stirring occasionally, until crisp, for about 10 minutes. Transfer to a paper towel-lined plate and set aside. Reserve 2 tbsps of bacon grease in the skillet and discard the rest.
3. Add the onion and bell pepper to the same skillet and cook, stirring occasionally, until soft and translucent, for about 10 minutes. Season with salt and pepper to taste.
4. Add the kale and cook, stirring occasionally, until wilted, for about 5 minutes.
5. Stir in the roasted sweet potatoes and bacon and spread the mixture in an even layer on the bottom of the skillet. Make four wells in the hash and crack an egg into each well. Season the eggs with salt and pepper to taste.
6. Transfer the skillet to the oven and bake for 10 to 15 minutes, or until the eggs are cooked to your liking.
7. Enjoy hot or at room temperature.

Nutrients (per serving)

Calories: 320   Protein: 16g   Fat: 16g   Carbohydrates: 28g   Fiber: 5g   Sugar: 8g

GREEN SMOOTHIE BOWL

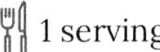 1 serving   🕒 5 mins    0 min

Dive into a vibrant green smoothie bowl packed with leafy greens, fruits, and a variety of toppings for added texture and flavor.

Ingredients

- 1/4 ripe avocado
- 1/2 cup fresh or frozen spinach
- 1/4 cup fresh or frozen kale
- 1/4 cup unsweetened almond milk
- 1 scoop vanilla protein powder
- 2 tsps sugar-free honey substitute
- A few ice cubes
- Optional toppings: unsweetened coconut flakes, hemp seeds, fresh berries, nuts, etc.

Instructions

1. Add all the ingredients to a blender and blend until smooth and thick. You may need to adjust the amount of almond milk or ice depending on the consistency you prefer.
2. Transfer the smoothie to a bowl and top with your favorite toppings. Enjoy!

Nutrients (per serving)

Calories: 280   Protein: 25g   Fat: 16g   Carbohydrates: 12g   Fiber: 6g   Sugar: 3g

EGG MUFFINS WITH SPINACH & FETA

 12 servings   🕐 10 mins   20 mins

Prep a batch of savory egg muffins filled with nutrient-dense spinach and tangy feta cheese for a quick and easy breakfast option throughout the week.

Ingredients

Cooking spray
10 oz (280 g) frozen spinach, thawed and squeezed dry
8 eggs
1/4 cup (60 ml) water
Salt and pepper, to taste
4 oz (110 g) feta cheese, crumbled

Instructions

1. Preheat oven to 375°F (190°C) and lightly spray a 12-cup muffin tin with cooking spray.
2. Chop the spinach and divide it evenly among the prepared muffin cups.
3. In a medium bowl, whisk the eggs and water until well combined. Season with salt and pepper to taste.
4. Pour the egg mixture over the spinach, filling each muffin cup about 3/4 full.
5. Sprinkle the feta cheese over the egg muffins.
6. Bake for 18 to 20 minutes, or until the eggs are set and lightly golden.
7. Enjoy hot or cold, or store in an airtight container in the refrigerator for up to 3 days.

Nutrients (per serving)

Calories: 90   Protein: 7g   Fat: 6g   Carbohydrates: 2g   Fiber: 1g   Sugar: 1g

CONTENT

1. Grilled Chicken Salad — 28
2. Turkey Lettuce Wraps — 29
3. Cauliflower Fried Rice — 30
4. Lentil Soup — 31
5. Greek Quinoa Salad — 32
6. Zucchini Noodles with Tomato Sauce — 33
7. Baked Salmon with Roasted Vegetables — 34
8. Black Bean and Corn Salad — 35
9. Tuna Salad Lettuce Cups — 36
10. Vegetable Stir-Fry with Chicken — 37
11. Spinach & Mushroom Stuffed Chicken Breast — 38
12. Quinoa and Vegetable Buddha Bowl — 39
13. Shrimp and Broccoli Stir-Fry — 40
14. Baked Cod with Lemon and Herbs — 41
15. Chickpea Salad with Cucumber and Tomato — 42

Grilled Chicken Salad

 4 servings  25 mins  10 mins

Ingredients

4 boneless, skinless chicken breasts

2 tbsps olive oil

2 tsps dried oregano

1 tsp garlic powder

Salt and pepper, to taste

8 cups mixed salad greens

1/4 cup sliced red onion

1/4 cup crumbled feta cheese

1/4 cup sliced black olives

1/4 cup chopped fresh parsley

1/4 cup lemon juice

2 tbsps olive oil

Salt and pepper, to taste

Nutrients (per serving)

Calories: 360

Fat: 22 g

Carbohydrates: 7 g

Fiber: 2 g

Sugar: 3 g

Protein: 35 g

Enjoy a satisfying and protein-packed salad featuring tender grilled chicken atop a bed of crisp greens and an array of colorful vegetables.

Instructions

1. Preheat a grill or grill pan to medium-high heat and lightly oil the grate. Cut the chicken breasts into thin slices and place them in a large ziplock bag. Add the olive oil, oregano, garlic powder, salt, and pepper and toss to coat well. Marinate for at least 15 minutes or up to overnight in the refrigerator.

2. Grill the chicken for about 4 minutes per side, or until cooked through and no longer pink in the center. Transfer to a cutting board and let rest for 5 minutes before slicing thinly.

3. In a large salad bowl, toss the salad greens with the onion, feta cheese, olives, and parsley. In a small bowl, whisk together the lemon juice, olive oil, salt, and pepper. Drizzle over the salad and toss to combine.

4. Divide the salad among four plates and top with the sliced chicken. Enjoy!

Turkey Lettuce Wraps

🍴 4 servings  10 mins  20 mins

Ingredients

1 tbsp oil

1 pound lean ground turkey

2 cloves garlic, minced

1/4 cup chopped onion

1/4 cup low sodium soy sauce

2 tbsps hoisin sauce

1 tbsp rice vinegar

1 tsp sesame oil

1/4 tsp red pepper flakes (optional)

8 large lettuce leaves (such as iceberg, romaine, or butter lettuce)

1/4 cup chopped fresh cilantro

Nutrients (per serving)
Calories: 250
Fat: 12 g
Carbs: 11 g
Fiber: 2 g
Sugar: 6 g
Protein: 26 g

Delight in a light and flavorful lunch by wrapping seasoned ground turkey in fresh lettuce leaves, creating a delicious and carb-conscious alternative to traditional wraps.

Instructions

1. Heat oil in a large skillet over medium-high heat. Add turkey, garlic, and onion and cook, breaking up the meat with a spatula, until browned and cooked through, for about 15 minutes. Drain any excess fat.

2. In a small bowl, whisk together soy sauce, hoisin sauce, rice vinegar, sesame oil, and red pepper flakes if using. Pour over the turkey mixture and stir to combine. Simmer until slightly thickened, for about 5 minutes.

3. Spoon about 1/4 cup of the turkey mixture onto each lettuce leaf. Sprinkle with cilantro and serve.

Cauliflower Fried Rice

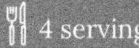 4 servings  10 mins  15 mins

Ingredients

4 cups riced cauliflower (fresh or frozen)

2 tbsps oil

2 eggs, beaten

1/4 cup chopped onion

1/4 cup chopped carrot

1/4 cup frozen peas

2 cloves garlic, minced

2 tbsps low sodium soy sauce

1 tsp sesame oil

Salt and pepper, to taste

2 tbsps chopped green onion

Indulge in a healthier twist on a classic Asian dish by substituting rice with cauliflower rice, mixed with an assortment of vegetables and savory flavors.

Instructions

1. Heat a large skillet over high heat and add one tbsp of oil. When the oil is hot, add the eggs and scramble quickly. Transfer to a plate and set aside.
2. Add the remaining oil to the same skillet and heat over high heat. Add the onion, carrot, peas, and garlic and stir-fry for about 5 minutes, or until the vegetables are crisp-tender.
3. Add the cauliflower rice and toss to combine. Stir-fry for another 5 minutes, or until the cauliflower is cooked through and slightly browned.
4. Add the soy sauce, sesame oil, salt, and pepper and stir well to coat. Stir in the scrambled eggs and green onion.
5. Serve hot or cold.

Nutrients (per serving)

Calories: 170

Fat: 12 g

Carbs: 10 g

Fiber: 3 g

Sugar: 4 g

Protein: 8 g

Lentil Soup

 4 servings  10 mins  45 mins

Ingredients

1/4 cup extra virgin olive oil
1 medium yellow or white onion, chopped
2 carrots, peeled and chopped
4 garlic cloves, pressed or minced
2 tsps ground cumin
1 tsp curry powder
1/2 tsp dried thyme
1 large can diced tomatoes, lightly drained
1 cup brown or green lentils, picked over and rinsed
4 cups vegetable broth
2 cups water
1 tsp salt, more to taste
Pinch of red pepper flakes
Freshly ground black pepper, to taste
1/4 cup chopped fresh flat-leaf parsley (optional)
Juice of 1/2 to 1 medium lemon, to taste

Nutrients (per serving)

Calories: 388
Fat: 14 g
Carbs: 51 g
Fiber: 18 g
Sugar: 12 g
Protein: 18 g

Warm up with a comforting bowl of hearty lentil soup, packed with fiber and protein to keep you feeling satisfied throughout the day.

Instructions

1. In a large pot over medium-high heat, warm the olive oil until shimmering. Add the onion and carrot and cook, stirring often, until the onion has softened and is turning translucent, about 5 minutes.
2. Add the garlic, cumin, curry powder and thyme. Cook until fragrant while stirring constantly, about 30 seconds. Pour in the drained diced tomatoes and cook for a few more minutes, stirring often.
3. Add the lentils, broth and water. Season with salt and pepper. Bring the mixture to a boil over high heat, then partially cover the pot and reduce the heat to maintain a gentle simmer. Cook for 25 to 30 minutes, or until the lentils are tender but still hold their shape.
4. Transfer 2 cups of the soup to a blender. Securely fasten the lid, protect your hand from steam with a tea towel placed over the lid, and purée the soup until smooth. Pour the puréed soup back into the pot.
5. Stir in the parsley (if using) and lemon juice. Taste and season with more salt and pepper if needed. Serve hot with crusty bread or crackers if desired.

Greek Quinoa Salad

 10 servings   15 mins  15 mins

Ingredients

2 cups water

1 cup quinoa

Pinch of salt

2 cups grape tomatoes, halved

1 English cucumber, chopped

1/2 cup pitted kalamata olives, halved

1/3 cup diced red onion

1/2 cup crumbled feta cheese

3 tbsps olive oil

3 tbsps red wine vinegar

2 cloves garlic, minced

1 lemon, halved

Salt and ground black pepper to taste

Nutrients (per serving)
Calories: 170
Fat: 11 g
Carbs: 16 g
Fiber: 3 g
Sugar: 3 g
Protein: 5 g

Experience the vibrant flavors of the Mediterranean with a refreshing salad that combines protein-rich quinoa, crisp cucumbers, juicy tomatoes, and tangy feta cheese.

Instructions

1. Bring water and quinoa to a boil in a saucepan. Reduce heat to medium-low, cover, and simmer until quinoa is tender and water has been absorbed, 15 to 20 minutes. Transfer quinoa to a large bowl and set aside to cool, about 10 minutes.

2. Mix tomatoes, cucumber, olives, onion, feta cheese, olive oil, vinegar, and garlic into quinoa. Squeeze lemon juice over quinoa salad, season with salt and pepper, and toss to coat.

3. Chill in refrigerator for 1 to 4 hours before serving or enjoy at room temperature.

Zucchini Noodles with Tomato Sauce

🍴 4 servings   🕐 10 mins   🔥 25 mins

Ingredients

4 medium zucchini

2 tbsps olive oil

Salt and pepper to taste

4 cloves garlic, minced

2 cups canned crushed tomatoes or

4 large ripe tomatoes, chopped

1/4 cup water

1/4 tsp red pepper flakes (optional)

1/4 cup chopped fresh basil

1/4 cup grated parmesan cheese

Nutrients (per serving)

Calories: 191
Fat: 12 g
Carbs: 16 g
Fiber: 5 g
Sugar: 10 g
Protein: 8 g

Savor a lighter and low-carb version of pasta by replacing traditional noodles with zucchini spirals, tossed in a flavorful tomato sauce.

Instructions

1. Wash and trim the ends of the zucchini. Using a spiralizer or a julienne peeler, make zucchini noodles and set aside.

2. In a large skillet over medium-high heat, heat olive oil and sauté garlic for about a minute, stirring frequently, until fragrant but not browned.

3. Add tomatoes, water, and red pepper flakes if using. Bring to a boil, then lower the heat and simmer for about 15 minutes, stirring occasionally, until the sauce is slightly thickened.

4. Add zucchini noodles and toss to coat with the sauce. Cook for another 5 minutes or until the zucchini noodles are tender but still crisp.

5. Stir in basil and season with salt and pepper to taste.

6. Sprinkle parmesan cheese on top and serve hot or at room temperature.

Baked Salmon with Roasted Vegetables

 4 servings   10 mins 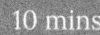 20 mins

Ingredients

4 (6-ounce) salmon fillets

2 tbsps olive oil

2 tbsps lemon juice

2 cloves garlic, minced

Salt and pepper to taste

2 tsps dried oregano

2 tsps dried thyme

4 cups broccoli florets

2 cups cherry tomatoes

1 large red onion, cut into wedges

1/4 cup chopped fresh parsley

Enjoy a nutritious and omega-3 rich meal by pairing perfectly baked salmon fillets with an assortment of roasted vegetables for a well-rounded lunch.

Instructions

1. Preheat oven to 400°F (200°C) and line a baking sheet with parchment paper.
2. In a small bowl, whisk together olive oil, lemon juice, garlic, salt, pepper, oregano, and thyme.
3. Place salmon fillets on the prepared baking sheet and brush with half of the oil mixture.
4. In a large bowl, toss broccoli, tomatoes, and onion with the remaining oil mixture. Arrange the vegetables around the salmon on the baking sheet.
5. Bake for 15 to 20 minutes or until the salmon is flaky and the vegetables are tender.
6. Sprinkle parsley over the dish and serve hot or at room temperature.

Nutrients (per serving)

Calories: 386
Fat: 20 g
Carbs: 16 g
Fiber: 5 g
Sugar: 7 g
Protein: 38 g

Black Bean and Corn Salad

 6 servings  10 mins  30 mins

Ingredients

1 (15-ounce) can black beans, rinsed and drained

2 cups frozen corn kernels, thawed

1 cup cherry tomatoes, halved

1 ripe avocado, peeled and diced

1/4 cup chopped fresh cilantro

2 tbsps olive oil

2 tbsps lime juice

1/2 tsp cumin

1/4 tsp chili powder

Salt and pepper to taste

Delight in a colorful and fiber-rich salad featuring black beans, sweet corn, and an assortment of crunchy vegetables, dressed in a zesty vinaigrette.

Instructions

1. In a large bowl, toss together black beans, corn, tomatoes, avocado, and cilantro.
2. In a small bowl, whisk together olive oil, lime juice, cumin, chili powder, salt, and pepper.
3. Drizzle the dressing over the salad and toss gently to combine.
4. Refrigerate for at least 30 minutes to allow the flavors to meld.
5. Serve cold or at room temperature.

Nutrients (per serving)

Calories: 215
Fat: 11 g
Carbs: 27 g
Fiber: 8 g
Sugar: 5 g
Protein: 7 g

Tuna Salad Lettuce Cups

 4 servings   10 mins  0 min

Ingredients

2 (5-ounce) cans tuna in water, drained and flaked

1/4 cup mayonnaise

1 tbsp mustard

1/4 cup chopped celery

2 tbsps chopped red onion

2 tbsps chopped fresh parsley

Salt and pepper to taste

8 large lettuce leaves

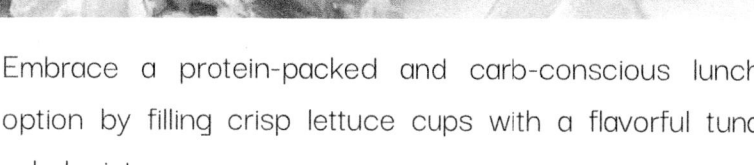

Embrace a protein-packed and carb-conscious lunch option by filling crisp lettuce cups with a flavorful tuna salad mixture.

Instructions

1. In a medium bowl, mix together tuna, mayonnaise, mustard, celery, onion, parsley, salt, and pepper.
2. Spoon about 1/4 cup of the tuna mixture onto each lettuce leaf.
3. Fold the lettuce over the filling and enjoy.

Nutrients (per serving)

Calories: 188

Fat: 11 g

Carbs: 3 g

Fiber: 1 g

Sugar: 2 g

Protein: 20 g

Vegetable Stir-Fry with Chicken

4 servings | 25 mins | 15 mins

Ingredients

1 pound boneless, skinless chicken breast, cut into thin strips

1/4 cup low sodium soy sauce

2 tbsps cornstarch

2 cloves garlic, minced

1 tsp grated ginger

1 tbsp sesame oil

2 cups broccoli florets

1 cup sliced carrots

1 cup sliced mushrooms

1/4 cup water

2 green onions, sliced

Nutrients (per serving)
Calories: 240
Fat: 7 g
Carbs: 15 g
Fiber: 3 g
Sugar: 5 g
Protein: 30 g

Stir-fry a medley of fresh vegetables and lean chicken in a fragrant sauce for a quick and nutritious lunch option bursting with flavors.

Instructions

1. In a medium bowl, whisk together soy sauce, cornstarch, garlic, and ginger. Add chicken and toss to coat. Refrigerate for at least 15 minutes or up to an hour.
2. In a large skillet over high heat, heat sesame oil and stir-fry chicken until golden and cooked through, about 10 minutes. Transfer to a plate and keep warm.
3. In the same skillet, add broccoli, carrots, mushrooms, and water. Stir-fry until the vegetables are crisp-tender, about 5 minutes.
4. Return the chicken to the skillet and toss to combine with the vegetables.
5. Sprinkle green onions on top and serve hot.

Spinach & Mushroom Stuffed Chicken Breast

🍴 4 servings 🕐 15 mins 🔥 30 mins

Ingredients

4 (6-ounce) boneless, skinless chicken breasts

2 cups fresh spinach leaves

1 cup sliced mushrooms

4 ounces cream cheese, softened

2 cloves garlic, minced

Salt and pepper to taste

1/4 tsp paprika

Nutrients (per serving)
Calories: 300
Fat: 14 g
Carbs: 5 g
Fiber: 1 g
Sugar: 3 g
Protein: 40 g

Dive into a wholesome and well-balanced lunch bowl featuring a vibrant assortment of cooked quinoa, roasted vegetables, and a drizzle of dressing.

Instructions

1. Preheat oven to 375°F (190°C) and lightly grease a baking dish.
2. Cut a slit in each chicken breast to create a pocket. Be careful not to cut all the way through.
3. In a small bowl, mix together spinach, mushrooms, cream cheese, garlic, salt, and pepper.
4. Stuff each chicken breast with about 1/4 cup of the spinach mixture. Secure with toothpicks if needed.
5. Sprinkle paprika over the chicken breasts and place them in the prepared baking dish.
6. Bake for 25 to 30 minutes or until the chicken is cooked through and the filling is hot.
7. Remove toothpicks and serve hot.

Quinoa & Vegetable Buddha Bowl

🍴 4 servings   🕐 10 mins   🔥 25 mins

Ingredients

1 cup quinoa

2 cups water

Pinch of salt

2 cups broccoli florets

2 cups cauliflower florets

2 cups cherry tomatoes

2 tbsps olive oil

Salt and pepper to taste

1 ripe avocado, sliced

1/4 cup hummus

1/4 cup tahini

2 tbsps lemon juice

2 tbsps water

Salt and pepper to taste

Nutrients (per serving)

Calories: 462
Fat: 28 g
Carbs: 46 g
Fiber: 13 g
Sugar: 9 g
Protein: 15 g

Delight in a colorful and fiber-rich salad featuring black beans, sweet corn, and an assortment of crunchy vegetables, dressed in a zesty vinaigrette.

Instructions

1. Preheat oven to 425°F (220°C) and line a baking sheet with parchment paper.

2. In a small pot over high heat, bring quinoa, water, and salt to a boil. Reduce heat to low, cover, and simmer until quinoa is fluffy and water is absorbed, about 15 minutes. Fluff with a fork and set aside.

3. In a large bowl, toss broccoli, cauliflower, and tomatoes with olive oil, salt, and pepper. Spread them in an even layer on the prepared baking sheet. Roast for 20 to 25 minutes or until tender and browned.

4. In a small bowl, whisk together tahini, lemon juice, water, salt, and pepper until smooth and creamy.

5. To assemble the bowls, divide quinoa among four plates or bowls. Top with roasted vegetables, avocado slices, and hummus. Drizzle with tahini dressing and enjoy.

Shrimp & Broccoli Stir-Fry

🍴 4 servings   ⏰ 25 mins   💧 15 mins

Ingredients

1 pound large shrimp, peeled and deveined

2 tbsps low sodium soy sauce

1 tbsp honey

2 cloves garlic, minced

1 tsp grated ginger

1 tbsp cornstarch

2 tbsps water

1 tbsp sesame oil

4 cups broccoli florets

1 tbsp sesame seeds

Nutrients (per serving)
Calories: 240
Fat: 7 g
Carbs: 16 g
Fiber: 3 g
Sugar: 8 g
Protein: 30 g

Enjoy a light and satisfying lunch by stir-frying succulent shrimp with crisp broccoli florets and a flavorful sauce.

Instructions

1. In a medium bowl, toss shrimp with soy sauce, honey, garlic, and ginger. Refrigerate for at least 15 minutes or up to an hour.
2. In a small bowl, whisk together cornstarch and water until smooth. Set aside.
3. In a large skillet over high heat, heat sesame oil and stir-fry shrimp until pink and cooked through, about 10 minutes. Transfer to a plate and keep warm.
4. In the same skillet, add broccoli and stir-fry until crisp-tender, about 5 minutes.
5. Return the shrimp to the skillet and stir in the cornstarch mixture. Cook until the sauce is thickened, about 2 minutes.
6. Sprinkle sesame seeds on top and serve hot.

Baked Cod with Lemon and Herbs

🍴 4 servings   🕐 10 mins   🔥 20 mins

Ingredients

4 (6-ounce) cod fillets

1/4 cup lemon juice

1 tbsp lemon zest

2 cloves garlic, minced

2 tbsps chopped fresh parsley

1 tbsp chopped fresh dill

Salt and pepper to taste

2 tbsps butter, melted

Delight in a tender and flaky baked cod fillet seasoned with aromatic herbs and brightened with a squeeze of lemon juice.

Instructions

1. Preheat oven to 400°F (200°C) and lightly grease a baking dish.
2. In a small bowl, whisk together lemon juice, lemon zest, garlic, parsley, dill, salt, and pepper.
3. Place cod fillets in the prepared baking dish and pour the lemon mixture over them.
4. Drizzle butter over the cod and bake for 15 to 20 minutes or until the fish flakes easily with a fork.
5. Serve hot with more lemon wedges if desired.

Nutrients (per serving)

Calories: 220
Fat: 9 g
Carbs: 3 g
Fiber: 0 g
Sugar: 1 g
Protein: 32 g

Chickpea Salad with Cucumber and Tomato

🍴 4 servings 🕐 25 mins 🔥 15 mins

Ingredients

1 (15-ounce) can chickpeas, rinsed and drained

1 large cucumber, diced

2 medium tomatoes, diced

1/4 cup chopped red onion

1/4 cup chopped fresh parsley

2 tbsps lemon juice

2 tbsps olive oil

Salt and pepper to taste

Enjoy a light and satisfying lunch by stir-frying succulent shrimp with crisp broccoli florets and a flavorful sauce.

Instructions

1. In a large bowl, toss together chickpeas, cucumber, tomato, onion, and parsley.
2. In a small bowl, whisk together lemon juice, olive oil, salt, and pepper.
3. Drizzle the dressing over the salad and toss gently to combine.
4. Refrigerate for at least 30 minutes to allow the flavors to meld.
5. Serve cold or at room temperature.

Nutrients (per serving)

Calories: 180

Fat: 8 g

Carbs: 22 g

Fiber: 6 g

Sugar: 5 g

Protein: 7 g

ENJOY MEAL

DINNER MAGIC

CONTENT

1. Grilled Chicken with Steamed Vegetables — 46
2. Baked Salmon with Asparagus — 47
3. Turkey Meatballs with Zucchini Noodles — 48
4. Stir-Fried Shrimp and Broccoli — 49
5. Oven-Roasted Chicken Breast with Cauliflower Mash — 50
6. Beef Stir-Fry with Mixed Vegetables — 51
7. Stuffed Bell Peppers with Ground Turkey and Quinoa — 52
8. Spaghetti Squash with Marinara Sauce and Lean Ground Beef — 53
9. Grilled Tofu with Roasted Brussels Sprouts — 54
10. Baked Chicken Thighs with Roasted Sweet Potatoes — 55
11. Cauliflower Pizza Crust with Veggie Toppings — 56
12. Mexican-style Chicken Lettuce Wraps — 57
13. Vegetable Curry with Brown Rice — 58
14. Greek-Style Grilled Lamb Chops with Greek Salad — 59
15. Zucchini Boats filled with Lean Ground Turkey — 60
16. Baked Eggplant Parmesan with Marinara Sauce — 61
17. Quinoa Stuffed Portobello Mushrooms — 62
18. Asian-style Stir-Fried Tofu with Bok Choy — 63
19. Ratatouille Stuffed Bell Peppers — 64
20. Lemon Herb Grilled Shrimp with Quinoa Salad — 65

GRILLED CHICKEN WITH STEAMED VEGETABLES

Enjoy a wholesome and protein-packed dinner featuring tender grilled chicken alongside a colorful assortment of steamed vegetables.

Nutrients (per serving)

Calories: 300

Fat: 11 g

Carbs: 12 g

Fiber: 4 g

Sugar: 5 g

Protein: 40 g

4 servings | 10 mins | 20 mins

Ingredients

4 (6-ounce) boneless, skinless chicken breasts

Salt and pepper to taste

1/2 tsp garlic powder

1/2 tsp onion powder

1/4 tsp paprika

2 tbsps olive oil

4 cups mixed vegetables (such as broccoli, cauliflower, carrots, green beans, etc.)

Water for steaming

Instructions

1. Preheat grill to medium-high heat and lightly grease the grates.
2. Season chicken breasts with salt, pepper, garlic powder, onion powder, and paprika on both sides. Drizzle with olive oil and rub the seasonings evenly.
3. Grill chicken for 15 to 20 minutes or until the internal temperature reaches 165°F (74°C), turning once halfway through.
4. Transfer chicken to a plate and keep warm.
5. In a large pot over high heat, bring water to a boil. Place a steamer basket over the water and add the mixed vegetables. Cover and steam for 10 to 15 minutes or until the vegetables are crisp-tender.
6. Serve chicken with steamed vegetables.

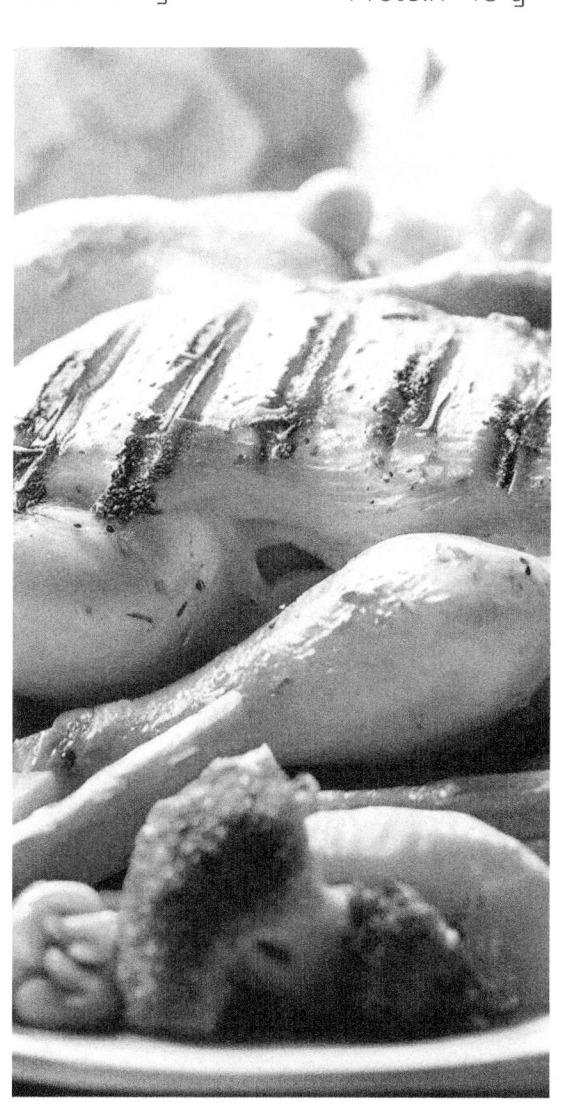

BAKED SALMON WITH ASPARAGUS

Indulge in a nutritious and omega-3 rich meal by baking succulent salmon fillets and pairing them with tender roasted asparagus.

Nutrients (per serving)

Calories: 360

Fiber: 3 g

Fat: 21 g

Sugar: 3 g

Carbs: 7 g

Protein: 37 g

4 servings   **10 mins**   **20 mins**

Ingredients

4 (6-ounce) salmon fillets

2 tbsps lemon juice

2 cloves garlic, minced

1 tsp dried dill

Salt and pepper to taste

2 tbsps butter, melted

1 pound asparagus, trimmed

Instructions

1. Preheat oven to 375°F (190°C) and lightly grease a baking dish.
2. In a small bowl, whisk together lemon juice, garlic, dill, salt, and pepper.
3. Place salmon fillets in the prepared baking dish and pour the lemon mixture over them.
4. Drizzle butter over the salmon and bake for 15 to 20 minutes or until the fish flakes easily with a fork.
5. In a large pot over high heat, bring water to a boil. Add asparagus and cook for 5 to 10 minutes or until crisp-tender. Drain and season with salt and pepper if desired.
6. Serve salmon with asparagus.

TURKEY MEAT BALLS WITH ZUCCHINI NOODLES

Delight in a lighter take on spaghetti and meatballs by replacing traditional pasta with zucchini noodles, served with flavorful turkey meatballs.

Nutrients (per serving)

Calories: 360

Fiber: 5 g

Fat: 18 g

Sugar: 12 g

Carbs: 24 g

Protein: 30 g

🍴 4 servings 🕒 15 mins 🔥 25 mins

Ingredients

1 pound ground turkey

1/4 cup breadcrumbs

1 large egg

1/4 cup chopped onion

2 cloves garlic, minced

2 tbsps chopped fresh parsley

Salt and pepper to taste

2 tbsps olive oil

2 cups marinara sauce

4 medium zucchini, spiralized into noodles

Instructions

1. Preheat oven to 375°F (190°C) and line a baking sheet with parchment paper.
2. In a large bowl, combine turkey, breadcrumbs, egg, onion, garlic, parsley, salt, and pepper. Mix well and shape into 16 meatballs. Place them on the prepared baking sheet.
3. Bake for 20 to 25 minutes or until the meatballs are cooked through and golden.
4. In a small pot over medium heat, warm the marinara sauce until simmering.
5. In a large skillet over high heat, heat olive oil and sauté zucchini noodles for 5 to 10 minutes or until tender but still crisp. Season with salt and pepper if desired.
6. Serve meatballs with marinara sauce over zucchini noodles.

STIR-FRIED SHRIMP AND BROCCOLI

Savor a quick and satisfying stir-fry combining succulent shrimp and vibrant broccoli florets in a savory sauce.

Nutrients (per serving)

Calories: 240

Fiber: 3 g

Fat: 7 g

Sugar: 8 g

Carbs: 16 g

Protein: 30 g

4 servings   25 mins   15 mins

Ingredients

1 pound large shrimp, peeled and deveined

2 tbsps low sodium soy sauce

1 tbsp honey

2 cloves garlic, minced

1 tsp grated ginger

1 tbsp cornstarch

2 tbsps water

1 tbsp sesame oil

4 cups broccoli florets

1 tbsp sesame seeds

Instructions

1. In a medium bowl, toss shrimp with soy sauce, honey, garlic, and ginger. Refrigerate for at least 15 minutes or up to an hour.
2. In a small bowl, whisk together cornstarch and water until smooth. Set aside.
3. In a large skillet over high heat, heat sesame oil and stir-fry shrimp until pink and cooked through, about 10 minutes. Transfer to a plate and keep warm.
4. In the same skillet, add broccoli and stir-fry until crisp-tender, about 5 minutes.
5. Return the shrimp to the skillet and stir in the cornstarch mixture. Cook until the sauce is thickened, about 2 minutes.
6. Sprinkle sesame seeds on top and serve hot.

OVEN-ROASTED CHICKEN BREAST WITH CAULIFLOWER MASH

Enjoy a classic roasted chicken breast served with a creamy and low-carb cauliflower mash for a comforting and nutritious dinner.

Nutrients (per serving)

Calories: 350

Fat: 17 g

Carbs: 12 g

Fiber: 4 g

Sugar: 5 g

Protein: 40 g

🍴 4 servings   🕐 10 mins   🔥 25 mins

Ingredients

4 (6-ounce) boneless, skinless chicken breasts

Salt and pepper to taste

1/2 tsp garlic powder

1/2 tsp onion powder

1/4 tsp paprika

2 tbsps olive oil

1 large head of cauliflower, cut into florets

2 tbsps butter

1/4 cup milk

2 tbsps chopped fresh parsley

Instructions

1. Preheat oven to 375°F (190°C) and lightly grease a baking dish.
2. Season chicken breasts with salt, pepper, garlic powder, onion powder, and paprika on both sides. Drizzle with olive oil and rub the seasonings evenly.
3. Place chicken breasts in the prepared baking dish and bake for 20 to 25 minutes or until the internal temperature reaches 165°F (74°C).
4. Transfer chicken to a plate and keep warm.
5. In a large pot over high heat, bring water to a boil. Add cauliflower and cook for 15 to 20 minutes or until very tender. Drain well and return to the pot.
6. Add butter and milk to the cauliflower and mash with a potato masher or an immersion blender until smooth and creamy. Season with salt and pepper if desired and stir in parsley.
7. Serve chicken with cauliflower mash.

BEEF STIR-FRY WITH MIXED VEGETABLES

Experience a savory and satisfying stir-fry featuring lean beef strips cooked with an array of colorful mixed vegetables.

Nutrients (per serving)

Calories: 280

Fiber: 4 g

Fat: 12 g

Sugar: 6 g

Carbs: 14 g

Protein: 30 g

4 servings | 25 mins | 20 mins

Ingredients

1 pound beef sirloin, thinly sliced

2 tbsps low sodium soy sauce

1 tbsp cornstarch

2 cloves garlic, minced

1 tsp grated ginger

2 tbsps vegetable oil

4 cups mixed vegetables (such as broccoli, carrots, snow peas, mushrooms, etc.)

Salt and pepper to taste

Instructions

1. In a medium bowl, toss beef with soy sauce, cornstarch, garlic, and ginger. Refrigerate for at least 15 minutes or up to an hour.
2. In a large skillet over high heat, heat oil and stir-fry beef until browned and cooked through, about 10 minutes. Transfer to a plate and keep warm.
3. In the same skillet, add mixed vegetables and stir-fry until crisp-tender, about 10 minutes. Season with salt and pepper if desired.
4. Return the beef to the skillet and toss to combine.
5. Serve hot.

STUFFED BELL PEPPERS WITH GROUND TURKEY AND QUINOA

Relish in vibrant bell peppers stuffed with a delicious mixture of lean ground turkey and nutritious quinoa, baked to perfection.

Nutrients (per serving)

Calories: 200

Fiber: 3 g

Fat: 9 g

Sugar: 6 g

Carbs: 14 g

Protein: 18 g

8 servings | 15 mins | 45 mins

Ingredients

4 large bell peppers (any color), halved and seeded

1 pound ground turkey

1 cup cooked quinoa

1/4 cup chopped onion

2 cloves garlic, minced

1 cup tomato sauce

1/2 cup shredded cheese (such as mozzarella or cheddar)

Salt and pepper to taste

2 tbsps chopped fresh parsley

Instructions

1. Preheat oven to 375°F (190°C) and lightly grease a baking dish.
2. In a large skillet over medium-high heat, cook turkey until browned and crumbly, breaking it up with a spatula as it cooks, about 15 minutes. Drain the excess fat.
3. In a large bowl, combine turkey, quinoa, onion, garlic, half of the tomato sauce, half of the cheese, salt, and pepper. Mix well.
4. Spoon the turkey mixture into the bell pepper halves and place them in the prepared baking dish.
5. Pour the remaining tomato sauce over the stuffed peppers and sprinkle the remaining cheese on top.
6. Bake for 25 to 30 minutes or until the peppers are tender and the cheese is melted.
7. Garnish with parsley and serve hot.

SPAGHETTI SQUASH WITH MARINARA SAUCE & LEAN GROUND BEEF

Discover a satisfying alternative to traditional pasta by using spaghetti squash, paired with a savory marinara sauce and lean ground beef.

Nutrients (per serving)

Calories: 250

Fiber: 4 g

Fat: 10 g

Sugar: 9 g

Carbs: 18 g

Protein: 23 g

6 servings | 15 mins | 75 mins

Ingredients

1 large spaghetti squash

1 pound lean ground beef

1/4 cup chopped onion

2 cloves garlic, minced

2 cups tomato sauce

1/2 cup shredded cheese (such as mozzarella or parmesan)

Salt and pepper to taste

2 tbsps chopped fresh basil

Instructions

1. Preheat oven to 375°F (190°C) and lightly grease a baking dish.
2. Cut spaghetti squash in half and scoop out the seeds. Place the squash halves cut-side down on the prepared baking dish and bake for 45 to 60 minutes or until tender.
3. In a large skillet over medium-high heat, cook beef until browned and crumbly, breaking it up with a spatula as it cooks, about 15 minutes. Drain the excess fat.
4. Add onion and garlic to the same skillet and cook until soft, about 10 minutes.
5. Stir in tomato sauce and bring to a boil. Reduce heat and simmer until slightly thickened, about 10 minutes. Season with salt and pepper if desired.
6. Using a fork, scrape the spaghetti squash strands into a large bowl. Toss with cheese and season with salt and pepper if desired.
7. Serve spaghetti squash topped with beef sauce and garnished with basil.

GRILLED TOFU WITH ROASTED BRUSSELS SPROUTS

🍴 4 servings   🕐 45 mins   🔥 40 mins

Enjoy a vegetarian dinner option with grilled tofu served alongside roasted Brussels sprouts for a flavorful and nutrient-dense meal.

Nutrients (per serving)

Calories: 300

Fat: 18 g

Carbs: 23 g

Fiber: 6 g

Sugar: 11 g

Protein: 18 g

Ingredients

1 (14-ounce) block extra-firm tofu, drained and pressed

1/4 cup low sodium soy sauce

2 tbsps maple syrup

2 cloves garlic, minced

1 tsp grated ginger

1 tbsp sesame oil

1 tbsp sesame seeds

1 pound Brussels sprouts, trimmed and halved

2 tbsps olive oil

Salt and pepper to taste

Instructions

1. Cut tofu into 8 equal slices and place them in a shallow baking dish.
2. In a small bowl, whisk together soy sauce, maple syrup, garlic, ginger, sesame oil, and sesame seeds. Pour half of the marinade over the tofu slices and reserve the rest for later. Refrigerate for at least 30 minutes or up to overnight.
3. Preheat oven to 400°F (200°C) and line a baking sheet with parchment paper.
4. Toss Brussels sprouts with olive oil and season with salt and pepper. Spread them in an even layer on the prepared baking sheet and roast for 25 to 30 minutes or until browned and tender.
5. Preheat a grill or grill pan over medium-high heat and lightly grease it.
6. Grill tofu slices for about 10 minutes per side or until charred and heated through. Brush with the remaining marinade as they cook.
7. Serve tofu with roasted Brussels sprouts.

BAKED CHICKEN THIGHS WITH ROASTED SWEET POTATOES

Indulge in tender and juicy baked chicken thighs served with roasted sweet potatoes for a well-rounded and satisfying dinner.

Nutrients (per serving)

Calories: 350

Fiber: 4 g

Fat: 18 g

Sugar: 9 g

Carbs: 24 g

Protein: 25 g

8 servings   **15 mins**   **50 mins**

Ingredients

8 bone-in, skin-on chicken thighs

Salt and pepper to taste

1/2 tsp paprika

1/2 tsp garlic powder

1/2 tsp onion powder

2 tbsps olive oil

4 medium sweet potatoes, peeled and cut into chunks

2 tsps chopped fresh rosemary

2 tsps chopped fresh thyme

Instructions

1. Preheat oven to 375°F (190°C) and lightly grease a baking dish.
2. Season chicken thighs with salt, pepper, paprika, garlic powder, and onion powder on both sides. Drizzle with 1 tbsp of olive oil and rub the seasonings evenly.
3. Place chicken thighs in the prepared baking dish and bake for 45 to 50 minutes or until the internal temperature reaches 165°F (74°C).
4. In a large bowl, toss sweet potatoes with the remaining olive oil and season with salt, pepper, rosemary, and thyme.
5. Spread them in an even layer on a baking sheet and roast for 25 to 30 minutes or until tender and caramelized.
6. Serve chicken with roasted sweet potatoes.

CAULIFLOWER PIZZA CRUST WITH VEGGIE TOPPINGS

Relish in a healthier twist on pizza by using a cauliflower crust topped with an assortment of colorful vegetables for a guilt-free and flavorful dinner.

Nutrients (per serving)

Calories: 180

Fiber: 5 g

Fat: 9 g

Sugar: 6 g

Carbs: 14 g

Protein: 13 g

4 servings | 15 mins | 40 mins

Ingredients

1 large head of cauliflower, cut into florets

2 eggs

1/2 cup shredded cheese (such as mozzarella or parmesan)

Salt and pepper to taste

1/4 cup tomato sauce

1/4 cup sliced mushrooms

1/4 cup diced green peppers

1/4 cup sliced black olives

2 tbsps chopped fresh basil

Instructions

1. Preheat oven to 400°F (200°C) and line a baking sheet with parchment paper.
2. In a food processor, pulse cauliflower until it resembles rice. Transfer to a microwave-safe bowl and microwave for 10 minutes or until soft. Let it cool slightly and squeeze out the excess moisture with a cheesecloth or a clean kitchen towel.
3. In a large bowl, combine cauliflower, eggs, cheese, salt, and pepper. Mix well and form a thin crust on the prepared baking sheet.
4. Bake for 20 minutes or until golden and firm.
5. Spread tomato sauce evenly over the crust and sprinkle with mushrooms, green peppers, olives, and basil.
6. Bake for another 10 minutes or until the cheese is melted and the toppings are cooked.
7. Cut into slices and serve hot.

MEXICAN-STYLE CHICKEN LETTUCE WRAPS

Embrace a light and flavorful dinner option by filling fresh lettuce leaves with seasoned chicken, salsa, and other Mexican-inspired toppings.

Nutrients (per serving)

Calories: 220

Fat: 8 g

Carbs: 7 g

Fiber: 2 g

Sugar: 3 g

Protein: 30 g

4 servings | **10 mins** | **20 mins**

Ingredients

1 pound chicken breast, cut into bite-sized pieces

2 tbsps taco seasoning

1/4 cup salsa

1/4 cup shredded cheese (such as cheddar or Monterey jack)

8 large lettuce leaves (such as romaine or iceberg)

Optional toppings: sour cream, guacamole, cilantro, lime wedges

Instructions

1. In a large skillet over medium-high heat, cook chicken with taco seasoning until browned and cooked through, stirring occasionally, about 15 minutes.
2. Stir in salsa and cheese and cook until cheese is melted, about 5 minutes.
3. Spoon chicken mixture onto lettuce leaves and top with your choice of toppings.
4. Fold the lettuce leaves over the filling and enjoy.

VEGETABLE CURRY WITH BROWN RICE

Dive into a fragrant and aromatic vegetable curry served with fiber-rich brown rice for a nourishing and flavorful dinner.

Nutrients (per serving)

Calories: 380

Fat: 9 g

Carbohydrates: 64 g

Fiber: 11 g

Sugar: 14 g

Protein: 13 g

4 servings **15 mins** **45 mins**

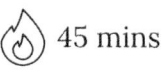

Ingredients

1 (13.5-ounce) can light coconut milk

2 tbsps red curry paste

1/4 cup water

1/4 tsp salt

1/4 tsp pepper

1 large onion, chopped

4 cloves garlic, minced

1 tbsp grated ginger

4 cups cauliflower florets

2 cups sliced carrots

1 cup frozen peas

1/4 cup chopped fresh cilantro

4 cups cooked brown rice

Instructions

1. In a small bowl, whisk together coconut milk, curry paste, water, salt, and pepper. Set aside.
2. In a large skillet over medium-high heat, cook onion, garlic, and ginger until soft, stirring occasionally, about 15 minutes.
3. Add cauliflower and carrots and cook until crisp-tender, stirring occasionally, about 15 minutes.
4. Stir in coconut milk mixture and bring to a boil. Reduce heat and simmer until slightly thickened, stirring occasionally, about 10 minutes.
5. Stir in peas and cilantro and cook until heated through, about 5 minutes.
6. Serve curry over brown rice.

GREEK-STYLE GRILLED LAMB CHOPS WITH GREEK SALAD

Enjoy a taste of the Mediterranean with juicy grilled lamb chops paired with a refreshing Greek salad for a vibrant and satisfying dinner.

Nutrients (per serving)

Calories: 400

Fiber: 3 g

Fat: 24 g

Sugar: 6 g

Carbohydrates: 12 g

Protein: 36 g

🍴 4 servings   🕐 45 mins   🔥 30 mins

Ingredients

8 lamb chops

1/4 cup lemon juice

4 cloves garlic, minced

2 tsps dried oregano

Salt and pepper to taste

2 tbsps olive oil

4 cups chopped lettuce

2 cups cherry tomatoes, halved

1 cup diced cucumbers

1/4 cup sliced black olives

1/4 cup crumbled feta cheese

2 tbsps red wine vinegar

Instructions

1. In a small bowl, whisk together lemon juice, garlic, oregano, salt, pepper, and 1 tbsp of olive oil. Pour half of the marinade over the lamb chops and reserve the rest for later. Refrigerate for at least 30 minutes or up to overnight.
2. Preheat a grill or grill pan over medium-high heat and lightly grease it.
3. Grill lamb chops for about 15 minutes per side or until the internal temperature reaches 145°F (63°C) for medium-rare or 160°F (71°C) for medium-well.
4. In a large bowl, toss lettuce, tomatoes, cucumbers, olives, feta cheese, vinegar, and the remaining olive oil and marinade. Season with salt and pepper if desired.
5. Serve lamb chops with salad.

ZUCCHINI BOATS FILLED WITH LEAN GROUND TURKEY

Delight in hollowed-out zucchini boats filled with a savory mixture of lean ground turkey and spices, baked to perfection.

Nutrients (per serving)

Calories: 300

Fiber: 4 g

Fat: 12 g

Sugar: 10 g

Carbohydrates: 16 g

Protein: 34 g

4 servings | 15 mins | 45 mins

Ingredients

4 medium zucchini

1 pound lean ground turkey

1/4 cup chopped onion

2 cloves garlic, minced

1 cup tomato sauce

1/2 cup shredded cheese (such as mozzarella or cheddar)

Salt and pepper to taste

2 tbsps chopped fresh parsley

Instructions

1. Preheat oven to 375°F (190°C) and lightly grease a baking dish.
2. Cut zucchini in half and scoop out the flesh with a spoon, leaving about 1/4 inch of the shell intact. Chop the flesh and set aside.
3. In a large skillet over medium-high heat, cook turkey until browned and crumbly, breaking it up with a spatula as it cooks, about 15 minutes. Drain the excess fat.
4. Add onion, garlic, and chopped zucchini flesh to the same skillet and cook until soft, about 10 minutes.
5. Stir in tomato sauce and season with salt and pepper if desired.
6. Spoon the turkey mixture into the zucchini shells and place them in the prepared baking dish.
7. Sprinkle cheese on top of each zucchini boat.
8. Bake for 25 to 30 minutes or until the cheese is melted and the zucchini is tender.
9. Garnish with parsley and serve hot.

BAKED EGGPLANT PARMESAN WITH MARINARA SAUCE

Savor a healthier version of a classic Italian dish by baking breaded eggplant slices layered with marinara sauce and cheese.

Nutrients (per serving)

Calories: 350

Fiber: 9 g

Fat: 16 g

Sugar: 12 g

Carbohydrates: 36 g

Protein: 18 g

4 servings | 30 mins | 35 mins

Ingredients

2 medium eggplants, sliced into 1/4 inch thick rounds

Salt and pepper to taste

2 eggs

1 cup breadcrumbs

1/2 cup grated cheese (such as parmesan or romano)

2 tbsps olive oil

2 cups marinara sauce

1/4 cup shredded cheese (such as mozzarella or provolone)

2 tbsps chopped fresh basil

Instructions

1. Preheat oven to 375°F (190°C) and lightly grease a baking sheet.
2. Sprinkle salt over both sides of the eggplant slices and let them sit for 15 minutes to draw out the excess moisture. Pat them dry with paper towels.
3. In a shallow bowl, whisk eggs with a pinch of salt and pepper. In another shallow bowl, combine breadcrumbs and grated cheese.
4. Dip each eggplant slice into the egg mixture and then into the breadcrumb mixture, shaking off any excess. Place them in a single layer on the prepared baking sheet.
5. Drizzle olive oil over the eggplant slices and bake for 25 minutes or until golden and crisp, flipping halfway through.
6. In a small saucepan over medium heat, warm marinara sauce until bubbly.
7. Spoon some of the sauce over each eggplant slice and sprinkle with shredded cheese.
8. Bake for another 10 minutes or until the cheese is melted.
9. Garnish with basil and serve hot.

QUINOA STUFFED PORTOBELLO MUSHROOMS

Experience a hearty and vegetarian dinner option with portobello mushrooms stuffed with a flavorful mixture of quinoa, vegetables, and herbs.

Nutrients (per serving)

Calories: 240 kcal
Fiber: 8 g
Fat: 11 g
Sugar: 7 g
Carbs: 30 g
Protein: 9 g

4 servings | 10 mins | 25 mins

Ingredients

- 4 large portobello mushrooms (stems removed, wiped clean)
- 1-2 tbsp avocado or melted coconut oil (or sub water or vegetable broth)
- 2 Tbsp balsamic vinegar
- 1/4 tsp each sea salt and black pepper
- 1/2 tsp smoked paprika
- 1/2 tsp cumin
- 1/4 tsp garlic powder
- 1/4 tsp onion powder
- 1/4 tsp oregano
- 1/4 tsp chili powder
- 1 cup cooked quinoa
- 1/2 cup cooked black beans (cooking/canning liquid drained)
- 2 Tbsp chopped fresh cilantro
- Juice of half a lime
- Optional: Magic green sauce or salsa for serving

Instructions

1. Preheat oven to 375 degrees F (190 C) and set out a baking sheet. Alternatively, heat a grill to medium-high heat and lightly oil it.
2. In a small bowl, whisk together oil (or water or broth), balsamic vinegar, salt, pepper, paprika, cumin, garlic powder, onion powder, oregano, and chili powder.
3. Brush the mushrooms with the marinade on both sides and place them gill side up on the baking sheet or grill. Reserve any leftover marinade for later.
4. Bake for 15 minutes or until slightly softened and juicy. Or grill for about 10 minutes per side or until grill marks appear and mushrooms are tender.
5. In a medium bowl, toss the cooked quinoa with black beans, cilantro, lime juice, and any remaining marinade. Taste and adjust seasonings as needed.
6. Spoon the quinoa mixture evenly into the mushroom caps and return to the oven or grill for another 10 minutes to heat through.
7. Serve with magic green sauce or salsa of choice if desired. Enjoy!

ASIAN-STYLE STIR-FRIED TOFU WITH BOK CHOY

Enjoy a delicious stir-fry featuring crispy tofu and vibrant bok choy, tossed in a savory Asian-inspired sauce.

Nutrients (per serving)

Calories: 250
Fat: 13 g
Carbs: 20 g
Fiber: 2 g
Sugar: 9 g
Protein: 16 g

4 servings | **10 mins** | **25 mins**

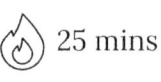

Ingredients

- 1 tbsp vegetable oil
- 1 (14-ounce) package extra-firm tofu, drained and cut into 1-inch cubes
- Salt and black pepper, to taste
- 1/4 cup low sodium soy sauce
- 2 tbsps rice vinegar
- 1 tbsp honey
- 1 tsp cornstarch
- 1/4 tsp red pepper flakes
- 2 tsps toasted sesame oil
- 4 cloves garlic, minced
- 1 tbsp grated ginger
- 4 cups chopped bok choy (or Chinese cabbage)
- Cooked brown rice, for serving

Instructions

1. Heat the vegetable oil in a large skillet over medium-high heat. Add the tofu cubes and season with salt and pepper. Cook for about 15 minutes, turning occasionally, until golden and crisp on all sides. Transfer to a plate and keep warm.
2. In a small bowl, whisk together the soy sauce, rice vinegar, honey, cornstarch, and red pepper flakes until smooth. Set aside.
3. In the same skillet over medium-high heat, heat the sesame oil. Add the garlic and ginger and cook for about 30 seconds, stirring constantly, until fragrant.
4. Add the bok choy and stir-fry for about 10 minutes, until crisp-tender and bright green.
5. Return the tofu to the skillet and pour the sauce over everything. Toss to coat and simmer for a few minutes, until the sauce is slightly thickened.
6. Serve hot over cooked brown rice.

RATATOUILLE STUFFED BELL PEPPERS

Experience a delightful twist on traditional stuffed peppers by filling bell peppers with a flavorful ratatouille mixture made with eggplant, zucchini, tomatoes, and aromatic herbs.

Nutrients (per serving)

Calories: 194

Fiber: 5 g

Fat: 11 g

Sugar: 10 g

Carbs: 15 g

Protein: 8 g

4 servings | 10 mins | 25 mins

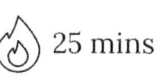

Ingredients

4 large bell peppers (any color), halved lengthwise and seeded

2 cups Ratatouille Provençal (see below)

1 cup shredded Italian cheese blend (4 oz.)

Chopped fresh parsley

Cracked black pepper

Ratatouille Provençal:

1/4 cup olive oil

2 cups coarsely chopped onions

2 cloves minced garlic

1/4 tsp salt

1/4 cup dry red wine

1/4 cup tomato puree (optional)

6 cups 3/4-inch pieces eggplant

6 cups 3/4-inch pieces zucchini

2-1/2 cups 1-inch pieces tomatoes

1 cup 3/4-inch pieces red bell pepper

3/4 tsp salt

Basil leaves (optional)

Instructions

1. Preheat oven to 425°F. Arrange pepper halves, cut sides down, in a 2-qt. rectangular baking dish. Bake for 10 minutes. Turn cut sides up.
2. For filling, in a medium bowl combine Ratatouille Provençal and 1/2 cup of the cheese; spoon into pepper halves.
3. Bake, covered, for 25 minutes or until peppers are tender and filling is heated through.
4. Sprinkle with remaining cheese. Bake, uncovered, for 5 minutes more or until cheese is melted.
5. Sprinkle with parsley and black pepper.

To make Ratatouille Provençal:

1. In an 8-qt. Dutch oven heat oil over high heat. Add onions, garlic, and salt; cook for 2 minutes or until onions are softened, stirring occasionally.
2. Stir in wine and tomato puree if desired. Cook and stir for 1 minute or until reduced by half.
3. Stir in eggplant, zucchini, tomatoes, bell pepper, and salt. Simmer, covered, for 10 minutes.
4. Simmer, uncovered, for 12 to 15 minutes more or until vegetables are tender and mixture is desired thickness, stirring occasionally.
5. If desired, top servings with basil.

LEMON HERB GRILLED SHRIMP WITH QUINOA SALAD

Delight in zesty and succulent grilled shrimp marinated in lemon and herbs, served alongside a refreshing quinoa salad.

Nutrients (per serving)

Calories: 435

Fat: 20 g

Carbs: 36 g

Fiber: 5 g

Sugar: 2 g

Protein: 30 g

🍴 4 servings   🕒 15 mins   🔥 25 mins

Ingredients

- 1 cup quinoa
- 2 cups water
- 1/4 tsp salt
- 1/4 cup chopped fresh parsley
- 2 tbsps chopped fresh mint
- 2 tbsps lemon juice
- 2 tbsps olive oil
- Salt and pepper, to taste
- 1 pound large shrimp, peeled and deveined
- 2 tsps lemon zest
- 2 tsps dried oregano
- 1/4 tsp red pepper flakes
- 2 tbsps olive oil
- Lemon wedges, for serving

Instructions

1. Rinse the quinoa under cold water and drain well. In a medium saucepan, bring the water and salt to a boil. Add the quinoa and reduce the heat to low. Cover and simmer for 15 to 20 minutes, or until the quinoa is fluffy and the water is absorbed. Fluff with a fork and transfer to a large bowl. Let it cool slightly.
2. Add the parsley, mint, lemon juice, and olive oil to the quinoa. Toss well and season with salt and pepper to taste.
3. In a small bowl, toss the shrimp with the lemon zest, oregano, red pepper flakes, and olive oil. Season with salt and pepper to taste.
4. Preheat a grill or grill pan to medium-high heat. Thread the shrimp onto skewers and grill for about 3 minutes per side, or until pink and opaque.
5. Serve the shrimp skewers over the quinoa salad, with lemon wedges on the side.

DESSERT BLISS

15 Mouthwatering Recipes

CONTENT

1. Mixed Berry Parfait — 68
2. Chocolate Avocado Mousse — 69
3. Greek Yogurt with Fresh Fruit — 70
4. Baked Apples with Cinnamon — 71
5. Chia Seed Pudding with Coconut Milk — 72
6. Strawberry Banana Smoothie — 73
7. Frozen Grapes — 74
8. Almond Butter Energy Balls — 75
9. Mango Sorbet — 76
10. Cottage Cheese with Berries — 77
11. Watermelon Fruit Pizza — 78
12. Blueberry Oatmeal Cookies — 79
13. Pineapple Nice Cream — 80
14. Dark Chocolate Covered Strawberries — 81
15. Pumpkin Spice Protein Bites — 82

MIXED BERRY PARFAIT

🍴 1 serving 🕒 5 mins 🔥 0 min

Indulge in layers of luscious Greek yogurt and a medley of fresh berries for a refreshing and guilt-free dessert.

Ingredients

1/2 cup yogurt

1/2 cup granola

1 cup mixed berries

Honey (optional)

Instructions

1. In a jar, layer yogurt, granola, and berries. Top with honey if desired.
2. Refrigerate up to 2 days. If you don't want soggy granola, wait until you're ready to eat the parfait to add it.
3. Enjoy!

Nutrients (per serving)

Calories: 457

Fat: 15 g

Carbs: 69 g

Fiber: 9 g

Sugar: 32 g

Protein: 14 g

CHOCOLATE AVOCADO MOUSSE

🍴 4 servings   🕐 10 mins   🔥 0 min

Savor a rich and creamy chocolate mousse made with the natural goodness of avocado, providing a satisfying and healthier treat.

Ingredients

2 ripe medium avocados, peeled and pitted

3/4 cup unsweetened cocoa powder

1/4 cup unsweetened almond milk

1/3 cup pure maple syrup

2 teaspoons pure vanilla extract

Pinch of salt

Nutrients (per serving)

Calories: 295

Fat: 18 g

Carbs: 40 g

Fiber: 14 g

Sugar: 20 g

Protein: 6 g

Instructions

1. Place the avocados in a food processor or blender and process until smooth and creamy, scraping down the sides as needed.
2. Add the cocoa powder, almond milk, maple syrup, vanilla, and salt and process again until well combined and no avocado lumps remain.
3. Transfer the mousse to a bowl and refrigerate for at least 2 hours or up to overnight, until chilled and firm.
4. Enjoy with fresh berries, whipped coconut cream, or shaved chocolate if desired.

GREEK YOGURT WITH FRESH FRUIT

🍴 1 serving   🕒 5 mins   🔥 0 min

Enjoy a simple yet delightful dessert by pairing creamy Greek yogurt with your choice of fresh fruits for a burst of natural sweetness.

Ingredients

3/4 cup plain Greek yogurt

1/2 cup mixed berries (such as strawberries, blueberries, and raspberries)

1 tablespoon honey (optional)

Instructions

1. Place the yogurt in a bowl and top with the berries. Drizzle with honey if desired.
2. Enjoy as a healthy and delicious breakfast or snack.

Nutrients (per serving)

Calories: 175

Fat: 0 g

Carbs: 30 g

Fiber: 4 g

Sugar: 24 g

Protein: 15 g

BAKED APPLES WITH CINNAMON

🍴 4 servings   🕐 10 mins   🔥 30 mins

Delight in warm and tender baked apples sprinkled with fragrant cinnamon, offering a comforting and wholesome dessert option.

Ingredients

- 4 large apples (such as Honeycrisp or Granny Smith), cored and sliced
- 2 tablespoons lemon juice
- 1/4 cup brown sugar
- 2 teaspoons ground cinnamon
- 2 tablespoons butter, cut into small pieces

Nutrients (per serving)

Calories: 250

Fat: 6 g

Carbs: 52 g

Fiber: 6 g

Sugar: 43 g

Protein: 1 g

Instructions

1. Preheat the oven to 350°F (177°C) and lightly grease a 9x13-inch baking dish.
2. Arrange the apple slices in an even layer on the prepared baking dish. Drizzle with lemon juice and sprinkle with brown sugar and cinnamon. Dot with butter pieces.
3. Cover the baking dish with aluminum foil and bake for 15 minutes. Remove the foil and stir the apples gently. Bake for another 15 to 20 minutes, or until the apples are tender and caramelized.
4. Enjoy as a warm dessert or a breakfast treat.

CHIA SEED PUDDING WITH COCONUT MILK

🍴 4 servings   🕐 5 mins   🔥 0 min

Dive into a creamy and nutritious chia seed pudding made with nourishing coconut milk, perfect for a satisfying dessert or snack.

Ingredients

2 cups light coconut milk

1/4 cup chia seeds

2 tablespoons pure maple syrup or honey

1/4 teaspoon pure vanilla extract

Pinch of salt

Fresh fruit for topping (optional)

Instructions

1. In a medium bowl, whisk together the coconut milk, chia seeds, maple syrup or honey, vanilla, and salt until well combined.
2. Transfer the mixture to a jar or an airtight container and refrigerate for at least 4 hours or overnight, until thick and pudding-like.
3. Enjoy with fresh fruit on top if desired.

Nutrients (per serving)

Calories: 200

Fat: 12 g

Carbs: 21 g

Fiber: 6 g

Sugar: 11 g

Protein: 4 g

STRAWBERRY BANANA SMOOTHIE

🍴 2 servings 🕐 5 mins 🔥 0 min

Sip on a refreshing and fruity smoothie combining sweet strawberries and creamy banana for a delightful and health-conscious dessert choice.

Ingredients

1 cup fresh or frozen strawberries

1 medium banana, peeled and sliced

1/2 cup plain Greek yogurt

1/2 cup milk or dairy-free alternative

Honey or maple syrup to taste (optional)

Instructions

1. Place all the ingredients in a blender and blend until smooth and creamy. Add more milk if needed to adjust the consistency.
2. Sweeten with honey or maple syrup if desired.
3. Enjoy as a refreshing and filling drink.

Nutrients (per serving)

Calories: 150

Fat: 2 g

Carbs: 27 g

Fiber: 4 g

Sugar: 17 g

Protein: 9 g

FROZEN GRAPES

🍴 Varies 🕐 20 mins 🔥 0 min

Enjoy a cool and naturally sweet treat by freezing grapes, providing a satisfying and refreshing dessert option.

Ingredients

3 cups red or white grapes

or as many as you want

Nutrients (per serving)

Calories: 62 per 100 g

Fat: 0 g

Carbs: 16 g

Fiber: 1 g

Sugar: 15 g

Protein: 1 g

Instructions

1. Rinse the grapes under cold water and drain well. Pat them dry with a paper towel and let them air dry for about 15 minutes.
2. Arrange the grapes in a single layer on a baking sheet lined with parchment paper or wax paper. Make sure they are not touching each other.
3. Place the baking sheet in the freezer and freeze for at least 2 hours or until the grapes are firm and frozen.
4. Transfer the frozen grapes to a ziplock bag or an airtight container and store in the freezer for up to 6 months.
5. Enjoy as a refreshing and low-calorie snack.

ALMOND BUTTER ENERGY BALLS

🍴 16 servings   🕐 10 mins   🔥 0 min

Relish in bite-sized energy balls packed with nutritious ingredients like almond butter, oats, and seeds, offering a convenient and satisfying dessert or snack.

Ingredients

- 1/2 cup natural almond butter
- 1/4 cup honey
- 1 teaspoon vanilla extract
- 1/4 teaspoon salt
- 1 cup rolled oats
- 1/4 cup ground flaxseed
- 2 tablespoons mini chocolate chips

Nutrients (per serving)

Calories: 112

Fat: 6 g

Carbs: 13 g

Fiber: 2 g

Sugar: 7 g

Protein: 3 g

Instructions

1. In a large bowl, stir together the almond butter, honey, vanilla, and salt until well combined and smooth.
2. Add the oats and flaxseed and mix well. Fold in the chocolate chips.
3. Shape the mixture into 16 balls and place them on a baking sheet lined with parchment paper. Refrigerate for at least an hour to firm up.
4. Enjoy as a healthy and energizing snack. Store the leftovers in an airtight container in the refrigerator for up to a week or in the freezer for up to a month.

MANGO SORBET

🍴 4 servings   🕐 10 mins   🔥 0 min

Indulge in a tropical delight with creamy mango sorbet, providing a naturally sweet and dairy-free dessert option.

Ingredients

3 large ripe mangoes, peeled and chopped

1/4 cup lime juice

2 tablespoons maple syrup or honey (optional)

Nutrients (per serving)

Calories: 150

Fat: 1 g

Carbs: 38 g

Fiber: 4 g

Sugar: 34 g

Protein: 2 g

Instructions

1. Place the mango chunks in a blender or food processor and blend until smooth. You may need to do this in batches depending on the size of your blender.
2. Add the lime juice and maple syrup or honey if using and blend again until well combined. Taste and adjust the sweetness and acidity as needed.
3. Transfer the mango mixture to a shallow baking dish and spread it evenly. Cover with plastic wrap and freeze for at least 4 hours or overnight, until firm.
4. Break the frozen mango mixture into chunks and return to the blender or food processor. Blend until smooth and creamy, scraping down the sides as needed.
5. Enjoy the sorbet right away or transfer to a freezer-safe container and freeze for another hour or so, until scoopable.
6. Store the leftover sorbet in an airtight container in the freezer for up to a month.

COTTAGE CHEESE WITH BERRIES

🍴 1 serving   🕐 5 mins   🔥 0 min

Delight in a protein-rich dessert by pairing creamy cottage cheese with a colorful assortment of fresh berries for a refreshing and nourishing treat.

Ingredients

1/2 cup low-fat cottage cheese

1/4 cup fresh blueberries

1 tablespoon chia seeds

1/4 cup walnuts (optional)

Instructions

1. Combine all ingredients in a bowl and stir well.
2. Enjoy as a healthy and filling breakfast or snack.

Nutrients (per serving)

Calories: 295

Fat: 18 g

Carbs: 22 g

Fiber: 9 g

Sugar: 10 g

Protein: 16 g

WATERMELON FRUIT PIZZA

🍴 4 servings   🕒 5 mins   🔥 0 min

Create a fun and refreshing dessert by using a watermelon slice as a base and topping it with assorted fruits, offering a vibrant and hydrating dessert option.

Ingredients

1 large slice of watermelon (about 1 inch thick), cut from the middle of the melon

4 tablespoons 0% Greek yogurt

2 large strawberries, diced

6 raspberries

10 blueberries

4 almonds, chopped

1 tablespoon desiccated coconut

Chocolate syrup (optional)

Fresh mint (optional)

Nutrients (per serving)

Calories: 51

Fat: 2 g

Carbs: 7 g

Fiber: 1 g

Sugar: 5 g

Protein: 3 g

Instructions

1. Place the watermelon slice on a large plate or platter and spread the yogurt evenly over it.
2. Sprinkle the diced strawberries, raspberries, blueberries, almonds, and coconut over the yogurt layer.
3. Drizzle with chocolate syrup if desired and garnish with fresh mint if using.
4. Cut into wedges and serve.

BLUEBERRY OATMEAL COOKIES

🍴 18 servings   🕐 10 mins   🔥 15 mins

Savor chewy and wholesome oatmeal cookies infused with juicy blueberries, providing a satisfying and fiber-rich dessert choice.

Ingredients

1 cup fresh or frozen blueberries

2 ripe bananas, mashed

2 cups quick oats

Nutrients (per serving)

Calories: 64

Fat: 1 g

Carbs: 13 g

Fiber: 2 g

Sugar: 4 g

Protein: 2 g

Instructions

1. Preheat oven to 350°F (177°C) and line a baking sheet with parchment paper or spray with cooking spray.
2. In a large bowl, stir together the blueberries and mashed bananas until well combined.
3. Add the oats and mix well until the oats are fully coated with the banana mixture. You should have a thick oat mixture that looks like cookie dough.
4. Scoop the dough with a cookie scoop or a tablespoon and drop onto the prepared baking sheet, leaving some space between each cookie.
5. Bake for 15 to 18 minutes or until the cookies are lightly golden and firm to the touch.
6. Let the cookies cool slightly on the baking sheet before transferring them to a wire rack to cool completely.

PINEAPPLE NICE CREAM

🍴 4 servings   🕐 10 mins   🔥 0 min

Enjoy a dairy-free and creamy "nice cream" made from frozen pineapple chunks, creating a tropical and guilt-free dessert experience.

Ingredients

2 ripe bananas, peeled and frozen

2 cups pineapple chunks, frozen

1/4 cup coconut milk

2 tablespoons maple syrup (optional)

Instructions

1. Peel and freeze bananas and pineapple chunks (preferably overnight).
2. When they are frozen, add both fruits to a high-speed blender or food processor.
3. Add in coconut milk and maple syrup if using, and blend on medium-high until you achieve a smooth, soft-serve consistency. You may need to stop and scrape down the sides occasionally.
4. Enjoy right away or transfer to a freezer-safe container and freeze for an hour or more for a firmer texture.
5. Scoop and serve with your favorite toppings.

Nutrients (per serving)

Calories: 157

Fat: 4 g

Carbs: 32 g

Fiber: 3 g

Sugar: 21 g

Protein: 1 g

DARK CHOCOLATE COVERED STRAWBERRIES

🍴 12 servings   ⏱ 20 mins   🔥 10 mins

Indulge in a classic and decadent dessert by dipping fresh strawberries in rich dark chocolate, offering a delightful and antioxidant-rich treat.

Ingredients

12 large strawberries, preferably long-stemmed

4 ounces dark chocolate (60% to 70%), finely chopped

1/4 cup lightly salted roasted pistachios, finely chopped

Nutrients (per serving)

Calories: 87

Fat: 6 g

Carbs: 8 g

Fiber: 2 g

Sugar: 6 g

Protein: 2 g

Instructions

1. Line a baking sheet with foil or parchment paper.
2. Place the chocolate in a heatproof bowl set over a pan of simmering water. Do not let the water boil or the bowl touch the water. Cook, stirring occasionally, until the chocolate has melted. Carefully remove the bowl and let the chocolate cool for 5 minutes.
3. Place the pistachios in a small bowl.
4. One at a time, hold a strawberry by the stem and dip into the chocolate, coating about two-thirds of the berry. Allow the excess chocolate to drip off, then dip into the pistachios. Place the coated strawberry on the prepared baking sheet. Repeat with the remaining strawberries.
5. Refrigerate until the chocolate is firm, about 10 minutes.

PUMPKIN SPICE PROTEIN BITES

🍴 18 servings 🕐 10 mins 🔥 0 min

Delight in bite-sized protein-packed bites infused with warm pumpkin spice flavors, perfect for a satisfying and seasonal dessert or snack.

Ingredients

- 1 cup gluten-free oats
- 1/4 cup almond butter or nut butter
- 1/4 cup shredded coconut, unsweetened
- 1/2 cup pumpkin puree
- 2 tablespoons honey
- 1/2 teaspoon vanilla extract
- 2 teaspoons pumpkin pie spice
- 1/4 teaspoon salt
- 1 scoop vanilla protein powder, gluten-free and dairy-free
- 1/4 cup chocolate chips, gluten-free and dairy-free

Nutrients (per serving)

Calories: 64

Fat: 3 g

Carbs: 8 g

Fiber: 1 g

Sugar: 4 g

Protein: 2 g

Instructions

1. Add 1/2 cup of the gluten-free oats into the food processor and blend until it turns into an oat flour. Then add in the remaining ingredients except the chocolate chips and pulse to combine.

2. Add in the chocolate chips and pulse a few times to combine, then use an ice cream scoop to scoop out the mixture. Use your hands to roll into balls.

3. Store in an airtight container in the fridge for up to a week or in the freezer for up to a month.

ENJOY MEAL

Printed in Great Britain
by Amazon